My Grown-Ups

Written by Kate Costigan

Illustrated by Sarah K. Turner

Halo
PUBLISHING
INTERNATIONAL

ISBN: 978-1-61244-993-7
LCCN: 2021905215

PUBLISHING
INTERNATIONAL

Hummingbird Humanity
an LGBTQ+ owned business

Halo Publishing International, LLC
8000 W Interstate 10, Suite 600
San Antonio, Texas 78230
www.halopublishing.com

Printed and bound in the United States of America

This book is dedicated to my mother, Heidi Ann Slade, my grandmother, Faith Fairman Conrad, and to all the grown-ups who helped make me, me.

Here we are together at last,
starting the year in our new class.

Some of us got here in buses;
some got here in cars.
Our teacher may have arrived
on a rocket ship from Mars!

No matter the way we got to our room, when we go home there is one thing we don't need to assume,

Our grown-ups will be there.

My grown-up was my grandma,
she really loved to eat.
My other grown-up was my dad,
who helped me make friends with
everyone on our street.

Slade's grown-ups are both girls.
One has straight hair; one has curls.

Leah met her grown-ups when she was three. They met her and knew she completed their family.

Rowan's grown-up is just one mom. She is very short and always calm.

Emerson's grown-ups are her grandma and grandpop. The fun in their house is always nonstop!

Niko has four grown-ups at
home and gets to stay with each
of them alone. Four grown-ups
in two different places—think
of all those smiling faces.

Miguel's grown-ups are named Abe and Brian. His family loves to dance and are always stylin'.

Lee's grown-up is his sister!
She came home from college to raise
him because he really missed her.

Your grown-ups at home might look different from mine, but that doesn't matter. That's AWESOME; that's fine!

Grown-ups come in all shapes, sizes, colors and ages. None of that matters, not in this story or out of its pages.

The thing that is most important
and true is that no matter
who your grown-ups are,
they take care of and love you.

CPSIA information can be obtained
at www.ICGtesting.com
Printed in the USA
BVHW021826230721
612734BV00005B/85